NEW VANGUARD ·

BRITISH HE[A]
CRUISERS 19[3]9–45

ANGUS KONSTAM   ILLUSTRATED BY PAUL WRIGHT

First published in Great Britain in 2012 by Osprey Publishing,
PO Box 883, Oxford, OX1 9PL, UK
PO Box 3985, New York, NY 10185-3985, USA
Email: info@ospreypublishing.com

Osprey Publishing is part of the Osprey Group

A CIP catalog record for this book is available from the British Library

Print ISBN: 978 1 84908 686 8
PDF e-book ISBN: 978 1 84908 685 1
EPUB e-book ISBN: 978 1 78096 430 0

Page layout by Melissa Orrom Swan, Oxford
Index by Sharon Redmayne
Typeset in Sabon and Myriad Pro
Originated by PDQ Media, Bungay, UK
Printed in China through Worldprint Ltd.

14 15 16 17 18   13 12 11 10 9 8 7 6 5 4

Osprey Publishing is supporting the Woodland Trust, the UK's leading
woodland conservation charity, by funding the dedication of trees.

www.ospreypublishing.com

CONTENTS

BRITISH HEAVY CRUISERS 1939–45

INTRODUCTION

When World War I ended Great Britain possessed the largest navy in the world. Many of these warships, and those still under construction, reflected the cutting edge of naval design and technology. Valuable lessons had been learned during the conflict and the Royal Navy's most modern warships reflected this hard-won wartime experience. The period from 1914 to 1918 was a heady time for naval designers, but during the two inter-war decades that followed few new warships were built and Britain eventually surrendered her maritime supremacy to the US Navy.

In naval affairs the inter-war years were dominated by a succession of naval treaties that set international limits on warship numbers, ship size and armament. In these circumstances it made sense to build new warships that met the upper limit of these international limitations. In the case of cruisers, this meant there was an international demand for vessels displacing 10,000 tons and armed with 8-inch guns. This led to the building of a new generation of British heavy cruisers, all equipped with these powerful weapons. During World War II these imposing warships formed the backbone of the Royal Navy's hard-pressed cruiser fleet.

The role of the cruiser was to protect maritime trade by hunting down enemy raiders, to support the main battle fleet by scouting for the enemy, defending it against attack by smaller torpedo-armed warships, and to maintain a calming presence overseas, particularly in the further reaches of the British Empire. Britain's largest heavy cruisers – known collectively as the Town class – were purpose-built to carry out these important tasks. These cruiser roles were in turn a modern version of the similar missions assigned to the frigates

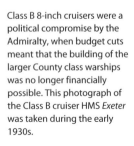

Class B 8-inch cruisers were a political compromise by the Admiralty, when budget cuts meant that the building of the larger County class warships was no longer financially possible. This photograph of the Class B cruiser HMS *Exeter* was taken during the early 1930s.

of Britain's sailing navy. While the way these ships looked and operated might have changed, their basic *raison d'être* remained the same for centuries.

The big difference of course was that by the outbreak of World War II the way naval campaigns were fought had altered dramatically. U-boats and aircraft were now a significant threat and this left Britain's now ageing fleet of heavy cruisers vulnerable to attack from above or below the waves. Consequently, as the war progressed these powerful warships found themselves increasingly sidelined and sent to theatres or made to perform menial duties where their lack of anti-air or anti-submarine defence was less of a problem. They were increasingly being asked to perform tasks for which they hadn't been designed, such as convoy protection, naval gunnery support and naval blockading. Strangely, the very factors that made them perfect for their original roles – long range and endurance, seaworthiness, the ability to function as squadron flagships, and a formidable degree of firepower – all ensured that they continued to play their part in the naval war throughout six years of bitter conflict. They remained useful naval assets – the unglamorous workhorses of the fleet – until the very end of hostilities.

The London class heavy cruiser HMS *Shropshire* as she appeared during the mid-1930s, when she was serving with the Mediterranean Fleet. In 1936 she was used to evacuate refugees from Barcelona as Franco's Fascists closed in on the city.

DESIGN AND DEVELOPMENT

During the period between the two world wars the cruiser was an important part of the fleet – probably the most highly visible and flexible component of the peacetime navy. This was largely because the cruiser was still needed to perform its primary functions of protecting maritime trade, showing the flag and helping to maintain order within the British Empire or in places where Britain maintained a trading presence. They were especially useful on the China Station where 'showing the flag' was deemed patricularly important.

There had been no heavy cruisers per se in the Royal Navy during World War I – only armoured cruisers and light, or protected, cruisers. These larger armoured cruisers had been designed to outgun all other cruisers, but they proved far less versatile than their designers had hoped and had effectively been rendered obsolete by the advent of the battlecruiser. The light cruiser was just that – a fast and lightly armed cruiser that performed all the traditional roles of the cruiser but which lacked the powerful armament of battlecruisers or older

armoured cruisers. By 1918 the remaining coal-fired armoured cruisers in the fleet were withdrawn from active service, leaving only the fleet of light cruisers, plus a new class of five large cruisers, which were still under construction. These new warships would represent a new departure for the British Admiralty. In effect, they would become the Royal Navy's first heavy cruisers.

Hawkins Class

During the opening months of World War I the German Navy tied down a disproportionately large portion of the British Fleet by using several of its cruisers as commerce raiders. The large cruisers of the Hawkins class were specifically designed to hunt down these types of commerce raiders and to counter the reported building of a new generation of large German cruisers mounting 170mm (6⅔-inch) guns. Their design was based on the Town class cruisers commissioned before the war, whose long range allowed them to fulfil their role of protecting the sea lanes and overseas possessions. However, the Hawkins class were bigger, faster and better armed than any of their predecessors.

The initial specifications called for a 9,000-ton version of the earlier cruisers, capable of achieving speeds of 30 knots. The proposed armament varied from 6-inch to 9⅖-inch guns, but after some deliberation the new 7½-inch Mark VI gun was selected, a powerful weapon with a maximum effective range of just over 21,000 yards (10½ nautical miles). With seven single mounts and a unified fire control direction system it was felt that these cruisers would be more than a match for any German cruiser they might meet. Another novel touch was that their boilers could be fuelled by either coal or fuel oil, which gave them greater flexibility when operating far from their normal bases. In effect they were purpose-built for the job of hunting down enemy warships wherever in the world they might appear.

The design was a sound one but by the time the plans were approved in 1915 the threat posed by German raiders had all but evaporated. Therefore while *Raleigh* was laid down that December, it was 1916 before work began on three of her sister ships, *Hawkins*, *Frobisher* and *Cavendish*. *Effingham* was laid down in 1917. By that stage it had been decided to complete *Cavendish* as an experimental aircraft carrier rather than as a cruiser and she finally entered service as HMS *Vindictive* in October 1918. Work on the rest slowed to a crawl, as resources were continually diverted to other ships. As a result, only *Hawkins* and *Cavendish* were launched before the end of the war, and by the time of the Washington Conference in 1921 only *Hawkins* and *Raleigh* had entered service as cruisers. *Frobisher* and *Effingham* would follow in 1924–25, by which time *Raleigh* had been lost through shipwreck off the coast of Canada. It was almost as if the navy didn't know what to do with these new cruisers. In fact, *Hawkins*, *Frobisher* and *Effingham* proved perfect

for showing the flag and for performing those other vital cruiser duties like protecting trade and maintaining order in distant outposts of Empire.

While these Hawkins class cruisers were an improvement on earlier vessels, they represented a compromise. They were armed with single guns, whereas by the 1920s the trend had moved towards the grouping of guns in turrets. A proposal to rebuild them to carry 8-inch guns in twin turrets came to nothing and so with some minor modifications they remained largely unchanged until the outbreak of World War II. They all had their coal-fired boilers removed during the 1920s, as the superiority of oil as a fuel had become apparent. During the 1930s *Frobisher* had two of her 7½-inch guns removed when she was converted into a training ship, but these were replaced at the start of the war. *Effingham* and *Hawkins* fared far worse and lost all of their main armament in 1937, prior to their conversion into 6-inch cruisers. They were eventually replaced by nine 6-inch guns and were redesignated as anti-aircraft cruisers. Thus, of the five Hawkins class cruisers, only *Frobisher* retained the firepower of a heavy cruiser.

The Washington Naval Treaty

By 1918 the great world powers had lost their appetite for building large battle fleets. Peacetime naval budgets would be significantly smaller than wartime ones and so it made sense to limit the size and composition of the world's navies. By reaching an international agreement future naval arms races could be avoided and governments could reduce their naval expenditure while still maintaining their national standing in terms of fleet size and quality. It seemed like the perfect solution for all concerned.

In November 1921 the Americans invited delegates from Britain, Italy, France and Japan to join them for a naval conference in Washington. There the various delegations tried to hammer out an agreement. The trouble was, every delegation had their own agenda. The Americans tried to impose a ban on the building of all new warships over 3,000 tons, apart from the replacement of vessels over 15 years old. The British rejected this, as most of their fleet was barely ten years old and would therefore risk being outclassed by their foreign rivals.

Like the other three extant cruisers of the Hawkins class, HMS *Frobisher* had been partly disarmed during the early 1930s and, while her sister ships were placed in reserve, she became a cadet training ship. She was re-armed in 1940–42 (see Plate E).

Then there was the problem of establishing treaty limits on warship size. Essentially this was set at the size of the largest warship any of the negotiating powers had in their fleet. In terms of cruisers this meant the British Hawkins class, displacing just under 9,900 tons and armed with 7½-inch guns. Therefore, the cruiser limit was set at 10,000 tons, carrying anything up to 8-inch guns. The number of warships of each type were also capped for each of the five powers, with the British and the Americans having parity in numbers (a tacit recognition of America's new post-war standing), with smaller quotas being agreed for the other three maritime powers (Japan, France and Italy). Britain was also permitted to build an extra handful of cruisers for the protection of trade, thereby continuing the Royal Navy's old role of guarding the sea lanes of Empire. The Washington Naval Treaty was duly signed in February 1922.

The British might have got a raw deal in terms of capital ship numbers, but in terms of cruiser fleets they got what they wanted. In fact, at an Imperial Conference in the summer of 1921, the Admiralty had proposed building a new class of post-war cruiser built around the 8-inch gun. They had already noted that there was a trend towards larger cruisers in America and Japan, and the British didn't want to be left out. The danger was of course, that all the signatories would soon begin building warships up to the treaty limits. This meant while 8-inch gun cruisers hadn't existed before, like them or not they would now form part of the world's major fleets. The term 'heavy cruiser' hadn't yet been coined – that came in during the 1930s. For now they were simply called 8-inch cruisers.

Therefore, even before the Washington Treaty was signed the Admiralty had been looking at proposals for a range of large cruisers, displacing between 7,500 and 10,000 tons apiece, and armed with four, five or eight 8-inch guns. The treaty simply meant that the design of these new cruisers could go ahead, and like their counterparts in other countries the British Admiralty would design their new warships up to their treaty limits.

As with any warship, their design would involve achieving a balance between protection, firepower, endurance and speed. The assumption was that these new cruisers had to be protected against the 6-inch guns mounted on most of their contemporaries – an approach that therefore left them vulnerable to other 8-inch gun cruisers. It was assumed that naval engagements would be fought at something close to maximum range – about 20,000 yards. Therefore, by concentrating armour around her vitals, as a means of protecting the ships against plunging fire, greater emphasis could be given to the vessels' armament and propulsion.

HMS *Hawkins* as she appeared in the summer of 1942 when she left to join the Eastern Fleet. Unlike her sister ships she regained all seven of her original 7½-inch guns, having been fully re-armed in Portsmouth during early 1942.

Endurance was also an important issue. These ships would be expected to cruise long distances, particularly as many of them would be earmarked for service in the Far East. Therefore they needed to be able to sail over 6,500 miles without needing to refuel. As the Director of Naval Construction (DNC) began looking at the problem, he realized that these ships couldn't merely be up-gunned versions of the Hawkins class. The design needed to be a unique one, to encompass all the requirements the Admiralty had specified.

It is worth noting that different navies approached the same problem in different ways. The Americans and the Japanese built cruisers with armoured belts, suggesting they planned to fight battles with them at close range. While the Japanese opted for twin turrets, the Americans preferred a more cramped triple turret. The Italians provided some belt armour, but concentrated on speed, while the French abandoned armour altogether. The British solution was a compromise, but one where endurance and reliability were given priority over protection and firepower.

HMS *Norfolk* as she appeared in late 1937, with the white hull and upperworks, and buff-coloured funnels and masts worn by British warships on the China station before World War II. She returned home shortly before the outbreak of war.

Kent Class

During the early 1920s the DNC was Sir Eustace Tennyson d'Eyncourt (1868–1941). He envisaged a type of cruiser with a flush deck and a high freeboard – a bit like the Nelson class battleships he was designing at the same time. In his view armour should be concentrated in a single protected deck at the waterline, to protect the ship's magazines and machinery spaces from plunging fire. In theory the large unarmoured hull could absorb a lot of damage without diminishing the vessel's capacity to sail and fight, while the armoured deck so low down in the ship also lowered her centre of gravity, making her less prone to capsizing through flooding. Unfortunately even this minimal degree of protection had to be scaled back, sacrificed for speed and firepower. This new class of ship also had to conform to the limits of the Washington Treaty.

The DNC left the more detailed design of these new cruisers to his subordinate, the constructor Charles Swift Lillicrap (1887–1960). Lillicrap drew up the plans and submitted them to the DNC for review in January 1923. D'Eyncourt insisted on a few modifications, but essentially the design was complete, apart from the fine detail. The finished plans were finally presented to the Admiralty the following October. Actually, d'Eyncourt presented three schemes, for cruisers armed with six and eight 8-inch guns, or with a smaller propulsion system in exchange for more armour. This was necessary as these new and largely unprotected cruisers represented a gamble in terms of the balance between speed, firepower and protection. In the end the Admiralty approved Lillicrap's plans and included them in their shipbuilding proposals for the tax year of 1924–25.

Having spent her first three years on the China station, HMS *Kent* returned home for a refit, when aircraft facilities were added. This photograph was taken in late 1931, after she resumed her duties in the Far East.

The Admiralty had worked out that it needed 70 cruisers to fulfil its strategic demands, but realized that building work would have to be staggered over several years, and even then post-war government parsimony meant that they would have difficulty pushing through the programme in an era of austerity and cuts. In the end, five of these new cruisers were ordered, while two more were authorized for service in the Australian Navy and paid for by the Australian government; these five British cruisers would eventually form the Kent class. They and their successors were also collectively, but informally, dubbed the County class.

Contracts were issued in the spring of 1924 and the first ship – the *Suffolk* – was laid down in Portsmouth Naval Dockyard that summer. The remaining four – *Berwick*, *Cornwall*, *Cumberland* and *Kent* would follow before the end of the year. Further modifications were made as the work progressed. For instance, engine power was reduced from 100,000 to 80,000 steam horsepower (shp), which meant a slight reduction in speed, but the weight gained could be used to provide a little additional armour. In the end the hull sides were provided with 1 inch of armour, rising to 2 inches around the machinery spaces, and 4 inches around the magazines. The waterline armoured deck remained just 1 inch thick over the engine rooms and 3 inches over the magazines. This was barely proof against 6-inch guns, let alone the guns of other 8-inch cruisers. While this protection was improved slightly after the Washington Treaty restrictions were lifted, ships of the Kent class remained poorly protected throughout their working lives. Their defence lay in speed and firepower, rather than in armour.

Kent Class					
Ship	**Builder**	**Laid Down**	**Launched**	**Commissioned**	**Fate**
Suffolk	Portsmouth Dockyard	30 July 1924	16 February 1926	7 February 1928	Broken up 1948
Berwick	Fairfield Shipyard, Clydebank	15 September 1924	30 March 1926	12 February 1927	Broken up 1948
Cornwall	Devonport Dockyard	9 October 1924	11 March 1926	6 December 1927	Sunk by Japanese aircraft, 5 April 1942
Cumberland	Vickers Armstrong Shipyard, Barrow-in-Furness	18 October 1924	16 March 1926	8 December 1927	Broken up 1959
Kent	Chatham Dockyard	15 November 1924	16 March 1926	25 June 1928	Broken up 1948

Despite delays in construction caused by labour disputes and supply problems, all five cruisers had entered service by the summer of 1928. They were earmarked for the China station, where their large profile and excellent range (over 9,000 nautical miles at 12 knots) made them ideal for service in the Far East. Although they proved useful additions to the fleet, they weren't without problems. It was found that smoke from the funnel eddied around the

open bridge and so their funnels had to be raised to alleviate the problem. Other modifications followed, such as the addition of an aircraft catapult and a High Angle Control System (HACS), to control anti-aircraft fire. Additional armour and 4-inch guns were also added in the years before the outbreak of World War II. *Cumberland* and *Suffolk* underwent major refits in 1935–36, when their quarterdecks were cut down to save weight. This was done for political rather than naval reasons, as it was found that their displacement had crept over the treaty limit. Essentially though, by 1939 these five cruisers had changed very little since they first entered service more than a decade before.

London Class

In late 1923 d'Eyncourt retired as the DNC and was succeeded by William J. Barry, an experienced naval constructor who had led the 8-inch cruiser design team. It was he who supervised the construction of the Kent class and who asked Lillicrap to develop plans for another batch of 8-inch cruisers. Barry and Lillicrap considered a few radical changes to their design. They investigated the use of triple gun turrets, which would add 400 tons to the finished vessel, but weight would be saved by sacrificing what little armour there was. This modification almost went ahead but it was discovered that there was simply no room to house the extra magazines without sacrificing engine space and therefore speed.

In the end the cruisers proposed for the 1925–26 round of funding were very similar to their predecessors. The biggest difference between the Kents and what became the London class was in protection. The torpedo bulge of the Kent class was omitted and additional armour was provided around the steering gear. The loss of the bulge also meant a slight increase in length and a decrease in beam was needed to maintain performance. The weight saved allowed Lillicrap to include an aircraft catapult in his initial design. The bridges were also set 15 feet further aft, to give A and B turrets a better field of fire.

ABOVE LEFT
HMS *Kent*, pictured in September 1941 shortly after emerging from a refit in Portsmouth. She carried this unusual scheme of grey-blue, light, medium and dark grey until 1944. During much of this period she operated in support of the Arctic Convoys.

ABOVE RIGHT
One of the initial problems with the design of the Kent class was that due to the large square fire control tower they carried, smoke from their forward funnels tended to eddy around the open bridge. In this pre-war view of HMS *Cornwall* the open bridge is covered by a canvas awning.

HMS *Suffolk* was extensively modernized during 1935–36, when like her sister ship HMS *Cumberland* her quarterdeck was cut down, giving these two cruisers a distinctive appearance. She is pictured here in 1937, before she underwent a last pre-war refit in 1939.

During the inter-war years HMS *London* resembled the other cruisers of her class. She is pictured here off Portsmouth in 1937 before undergoing the major rebuilding work (1939–41) that would completely transform her appearance and impair her performance.

Another modification was the rearrangement of the machinery spaces, to permit increased watertight sub-division – of vital importance if the vessel was ever hit by a torpedo. This also reduced the risk of a single hit knocking out the ship's machinery. Approval was given for four new vessels, which duly became the London class. The first of them – the *London* – was laid down in early 1927 and, although two were delayed a year due to funding problems, all four had entered service by the autumn of 1929.

Plans were laid to modify these four ships during the 1930s, but apart from HACS being added, and changes made to their secondary armament and catapult systems, only *London* underwent any major changes before 1939. When the war broke out she was already undergoing a major refit in Chatham and by the time she emerged in 1941 she was virtually

London Class					
Ship	Builder	Laid Down	Launched	Commissioned	Fate
London	Portsmouth Dockyard	23 February 1926	14 September 1927	31 January 1929	Broken up 1950
Devonshire	Devonport Dockyard	16 March 1926	22 October 1927	18 March 1929	Broken up 1954
Sussex	Hawthorne Leslie Shipyard, Tyneside	1 February 1927	22 February 1928	19 March 1929	Broken up 1955
Shropshire	Beardmore Shipyard, Clydeside	24 February 1927	5 July 1928	12 September 1929	Broken up 1955

unrecognizable. One of her funnels had been lost, her bridge was greatly enlarged and she received minor modifications to her armament and aircraft

 HMS *CUMBERLAND* (1940) AND HMS *SUFFOLK* (1941)

HMS *Cumberland* (top) is depicted as she looked while operating off the Vichy French port of Dakar in September 1940. On 23 September she was hit by a 125mm shell fired by a coastal battery, which forced her to withdraw from the action. She retained this unofficial two-colour disruptive scheme until she returned to Britain for a refit in July 1941. She was then repainted in a more conventional Admiralty disruptive scheme of blue-grey, medium and dark grey over a light-grey base. Her decks remained unpainted.

HMS *Suffolk* (bottom) is portrayed as she appeared during the shadowing of the German battleship *Bismarck* in May 1941, operating in company with HMS *Norfolk*. She sports a variant of the Admiralty disruptive scheme, with grey-green and dark grey painted over a light-grey base. During this war her decks were painted dark grey. *Suffolk* retained this striking camouflage scheme from February 1941 to March 1942. When she emerged from her next refit in July 1942 she wore the latest version of the Admiralty disruptive scheme of medium and dark grey over a light-grey base. She retained this new scheme until the following April.

facilities. These changes were not a success – the added weight placed a strain on her hull and she needed a second wartime refit before she was deemed fully operational. With these modifications she looked similar to the Fiji (or Colony) class of light cruisers that were being built around the same time. *London's* sister ships retained the look of their County class contemporaries.

HMS *Shropshire* at anchor in Scapa Flow in August 1941. She lies in a nearly deserted main fleet anchorage, protected by a line of anti-torpedo nets maintained by a handful of steam drifters. Two months later she was sent to Chatham, Kent for a refit, and in early 1943 she was handed over to the Royal Australian Navy.

Norfolk Class

The Admiralty planned to include three additional cruisers in their funding programme for 1926–27, one of which would be a small 8-inch cruiser carrying just six guns. The remaining two were intended to be repeats of the London class, as in order to keep the cruiser programme on schedule tenders had to be issued before the autumn of 1926. An improved type of 8-inch gun mount was used (the Mark II turret), while new methods of steel production allowed a little more weight to be used to increase the vessels' armoured protection. During the summer of 1926 various armour configurations were considered, but none proved satisfactory. Essentially, providing adequate protection against 6-inch and 8-inch guns was impossible if the ships were to be built within the Washington Treaty limit of 10,000 tons. Therefore the last two warships of the County class retained the same armoured protection as their predecessors, with only minor improvements.

These two eight-gun 8-inch cruisers became the Norfolk class. Two more Norfolk class cruisers, *Northumberland* and *Surrey*, were ordered in the summer of 1929, to be built in Portsmouth and Devonport, but a combination of a change of government and the Wall Street Crash led to their cancellation in January 1930. Both of the remaining cruisers – *Norfolk* and *Devonshire* – underwent minor modifications during the 1930s, with new HACS and anti-aircraft guns fitted, together with a new aircraft catapult and an improved bridge. In terms of appearance they were virtually identical to the London class, although they were both fitted with a modern Director Control Tower (DCT) on top of the bridge, which replaced the smaller square box fitted to earlier Counties.

Norfolk Class					
Ship	Builder	Laid Down	Launched	Commissioned	Fate
Norfolk	Fairfield Shipyard, Clydebank	8 July 1927	12 December 1928	30 April 1930	Broken up 1950
Dorsetshire	Portsmouth Dockyard	21 September 1927	29 January 1929	30 September 1930	Sunk by Japanese aircraft, 5 April 1942

The Norfolk class represented the final development of the Class A, or County class, 8-inch cruisers. This pre-war image of HMS *Norfolk* shows the modern director control tower fitted on top of her bridge. Earlier 8-inch cruisers had a smaller, square-shaped control tower.

Class B Cruisers

In early 1925 Barry asked Lillicrap to develop plans for smaller 6-inch gun cruisers, but based on the designs for the County class. The hull shape had to be modified and was more like those of the Hawkins class, but what Lillicrap produced was a plan for a 6,000-ton cruiser that was faster and sleeker than its 8-inch predecessors. Lillicrap based his design around a cruiser with eight 6-inch guns in four twin turrets, but he also considered other configurations, one of which was for six 8-inch guns.

In the end it was political rather than naval considerations that forced the Admiralty to consider Lillicrap's small 8-inch cruiser design. The British government was under pressure to reduce its expenditure on Imperial defence and so the Admiralty found itself starved of the funds it needed to reach its target of 70 modern cruisers. Lillicrap's design offered a cheaper alternative to the costly County class and in December 1925 the Admiralty approved plans for what they called a Class B cruiser. In effect it would be a three-turret version of the County class (now dubbed Class A). Lillicrap's final plan was for an 8,200-ton ship which could match the larger cruisers in terms of range and speed but which enjoyed slightly better protection, with 3-inch side armour over its machinery spaces and 4⅜ inches over its magazines. Waterline deck armour offered protection to these vital areas similar to that of the larger cruisers of the London class. The Class B cruiser had its two forward funnels trunked together, producing a rather inelegant arrangement of two funnels, one larger than the other.

The first of these new cruisers – the *York* – was laid down in 1927 and entered service three years later. Two cruisers had been planned for the class but due to financial restraints one of them – the *Exeter* – was delayed until the following fiscal year. In the interim several modifications were made to the design, including improved protection around the magazines, a more streamlined bridge structure, and a modified aircraft catapult, allowing two aircraft to be carried. During the 1930s *York* had her catapult replaced and extra anti-aircraft guns added. *Exeter* was also given extra anti-aircraft machine guns, but essentially the two ships entered World War II looking pretty much the same as they had when they first entered service.

HMS *Dorsetshire*, displaying the camouflage scheme she carried from the first months of 1941 until at least the start of 1942. She carried a mirror image of the scheme on her port side and her wooden decks remained unpainted.

Class B Cruisers					
Ship	Builder	Laid Down	Launched	Commissioned	Fate
York	Palmers Shipyard, Tyneside	16 May 1927	17 July 1928	1 May 1930	Sunk by Italian torpedo boats, 26 March 1941
Exeter	Devonport Dockyard	1 August 1928	18 July 1929	27 July 1931	Sunk by Japanese task force, 1 March 1942

While the Class B cruisers lacked the spacious hulls of other British 8-inch cruisers, particularly as they were both stepped down towards the stern, they proved excellent sea boats and useful additions to the fleet, where their principal peacetime role was to show the flag in the West Indies station and with the Mediterranean Fleet. This role of 'showing the flag' was one that these 8-inchers were well suited for, particularly the Counties with their imposing high freeboard, spacious hulls and magisterial presence. They were the perfect guardians of the inter-war Pax Britannica. Just how they would fare in action had still to be discovered.

Like the Norfolk class cruisers commissioned before her, HMS *York*, the first of two Type B 8-inch cruisers, was fitted with a modern director control tower, designed to improve her gunnery performance. She is pictured here in 1930, but her appearance was hardly changed before her loss in March 1931.

HMS *NORFOLK* (1941) AND HMS *YORK* (1941)

In May 1941 HMS *Norfolk* (top) flew the flag of Rear-Admiral Wake-Walker, the commander of the 1st Cruiser Squadron. Operating in consort with HMS *Suffolk*, Wake-Walker's flagship shadowed the *Bismarck* and *Prinz Eugen* during the night of 23–24 May, sending regular reports to Admiral Holland in *Hood*, and to the Admiralty. After the loss of *Hood* the following morning, *Norfolk* and *Suffolk* kept their distance from the enemy, but used their radar to shadow the German warships as they headed south into the North Atlantic. She is shown in the camouflage pattern she wore at the time. Her decks and turret tops were painted a dark blue.

HMS *York* (bottom) is shown as she appeared from February 1940 until her final destruction at Suda Bay in Crete in May 1941. Her port side camouflage arrangement was virtually a mirror image of the starboard side shown here. Before her 1939–40 refit she was painted in an overall medium grey. Essentially this scheme was one approved for use in the Home Fleet. The opportunity to repaint her in the Alexandria-pattern camouflage favoured in the Mediterranean Fleet never presented itself.

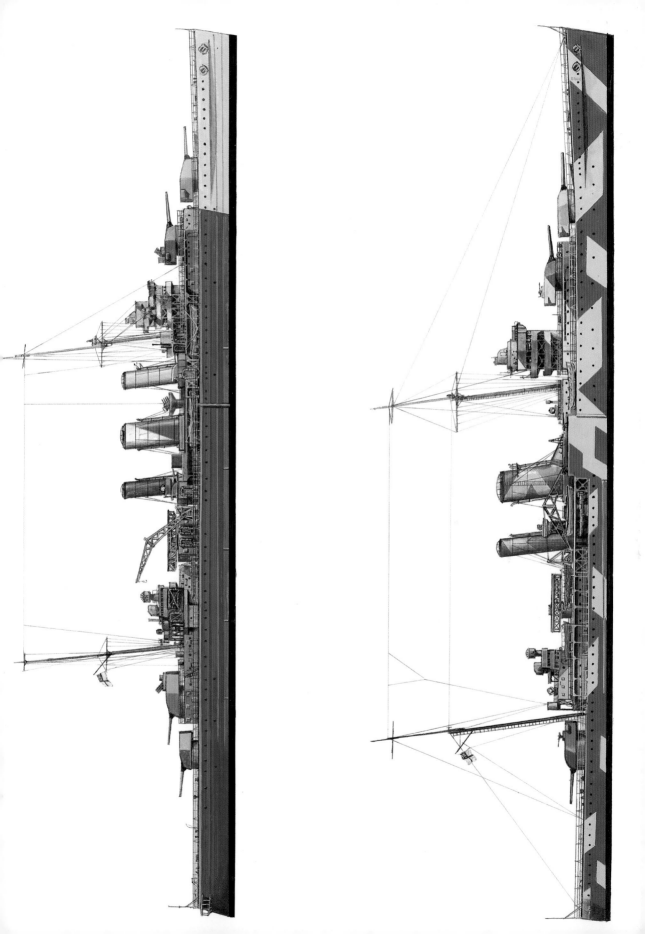

The Kent class heavy cruiser HMS *Berwick* undergoing a minor refit in Rosyth Dockyard on the Firth of Forth, during the late summer of 1943. During her visit she had her close-range AA weaponry and radar suite updated, and her aircraft facilities removed.

HEAVY CRUISER SPECIFICATIONS, SEPTEMBER 1939

Hawkins Class

Displacement	9,860 tons (standard)
Dimensions Length Beam Draught	 605ft overall 65ft 17ft 3in.
Propulsion	4 Brown-Curtis turbines, 12 Yarrow boilers, producing 65,000shp (Note: *Hawkins* fitted with Parsons turbines and 12 boilers, producing 55,000shp)
Maximum speed	30½kn (*Hawkins*: 29½kn)
Fuel oil capacity	2,186 tons (*Hawkins*: 2,600 tons)
Range	5,400 miles at 14kn
Aircraft	None fitted (although catapult fitted to *Frobisher*)
Armour Belt Decks Conning tower Magazines	 1½–3in. 1–1½in. 3in. ½–1in.
Complement	690 officers and men

Armament

Hawkins	4 x 4in. Mk V QF guns in single mounts 2 x 2-pdrs in single mounts 2 x 21in. torpedoes in single underwater mounts
Frobisher	5 x 7½in. Mk VI BL guns in single turrets 2 x 4in. Mk V QF guns in single mounts 2 x 2-pdrs in single mounts 6 x 21in. torpedoes, 2 in single underwater mounts, 4 in 2 x twin mounts
Effingham	9 x 6in. Mk XII BL guns in single mounts, 4 x 4in. Mk V QF guns in single mounts 12 x ½in. MGs in 3 quadruple mounts

Wartime Modifications

Hawkins	January 1940: 4 x single 2-pdrs added. May 1942: 2 x quad 2-pdr pom-poms added; 7 x single 20mm added; 2 x single 2-pdrs removed; Type 273, 281 and 285 radars added. August 1944: quad 2-pdrs replaced by 8-barrelled versions; 2 x single 20mm added.
Frobisher	March 1942: 3 x single 4in. AA guns added; 4 x quad 2-pdr pom-poms added; 2 x single 2-pdrs removed; 7 x single 20mm added; Type 273, 281 and 285 radars added. May 1944: 2 quad 2-pdrs replaced by 8-barrelled versions; 12 x single 20mm added.
Effingham	None

Kent Class

Displacement	10,900 tons (standard)
Dimensions Length Beam Draught	630ft overall 68ft 5in. 20ft 6in.
Propulsion	4 Parsons turbines, 8 Admiralty boilers, producing 80,000shp (Note: *Berwick* fitted with Brown-Curtis turbines)
Maximum speed	31½kn
Fuel oil capacity	3,424 tons
Range	9,350 miles at 12kn
Aircraft	One (Walrus) – two occasionally carried
Armour Belt Decks Turrets	1in. 1–4½in. around magazines 1in.
Complement	784 officers and men

Armament

Berwick	8 x 8in. Mk VIII BL guns in twin turrets 8 x 4in. Mk V QF guns in twin mounts 2 x 8-barrelled 2-pdrs 8 x 21in. torpedoes in two quadruple mounts 2 x quad ½in. MGs
Cornwall	8 x 8in. Mk VIII BL guns in twin turrets 8 x 4in. Mk V QF guns in twin mounts 2 x 8-barrelled 2-pdrs 8 x 21in. torpedoes in two quadruple mounts 2 x quad ½in. MGs
Cumberland	8 x 8in. Mk VIII BL guns in twin turrets 6 x 4in. in 2 single and 2 twin mounts 2 x quad 2-pdrs 2 x quad ½in. MGs
Kent	8 x 8in. Mk VIII BL guns in twin turrets 5 x single 4in. 2 x 8-barrelled 2-pdrs 8 x 21in. torpedoes in two quadruple mounts 2 x quad ½in. MGs
Suffolk	8 x 8in. Mk VIII BL guns in twin turrets 4 x 4in. in single mounts 2 x quad 2-pdrs 2 x quad ½in. MGs

Wartime Modifications

Berwick	April 1941: 5 x single 20mm added; Type 284M and 286 radars added. July 1942: quad MGs removed; 6 x single 20mm added; aircraft and catapult removed; Type 273, 279 and 283 radar added. October 1943: 7 x single 20mm replaced by twin 20mm; Type 279 radar removed, type 281B, 283 and 285 radar added. March 1944: 2 x single 20mm removed.
Cornwall	None
Cumberland	September 1941: 5 x single 20mm added; Type 281, 285 and 272 radar added. May 1943: quad MGs and 1 x single 20mm removed; 5 x twin 20mm added. August 1943: aircraft and catapult removed; Type 282 radar added. February 1945: 2 x single 20mm added.
Kent	August 1941: 6 x single 20mm added; Type 281, 284 and 285 radar added. October 1942: aircraft and catapult removed; type 273 radar added; quad MGs replaced by 6 x single 20mm. September 1943: 6 x single 20mm replaced by 3 x twin 20mm; Type 283 radar added.
Suffolk	December 1940: 2 x 4in. in twin mounts replaced 2 x 4in. in single mounts; 4 x single 20mm added; Type 279, 284 and 285 radars added. June 1942: quad MGs removed; 4 x single 20mm added; Type 279 radar removed; Type 273 and 281 radar added. January 1943: Aircraft and catapult removed; Type 282 radar added; 5 x single 20mm replaced by 5 x twin 20mm. March 1943: 3 x single 20mm added.

During much of 1940 HMS *Exeter* underwent an extensive refit in Devonport, when her single 4-inch guns were replaced by twin mounts, her double catapult was replaced by a larger single one, and she was fitted with radar. She is pictured here in May 1941, shortly after her return to service.

York Class

Displacement	8,250 tons (standard)
Dimensions Length Beam Draught	 575ft overall 57ft 20ft 3in.
Propulsion	4 Parsons turbines, 8 Admiralty boilers, producing 80,000shp
Maximum speed	32kn
Fuel oil capacity	1,900 tons
Range	10,000 miles at 14kn
Aircraft	One (Walrus)
Armour Belt Decks Turrets	 1in. 1–5in. around magazines 1in.
Complement	628 officers and men
Armament	
York	6 x 8in. Mk VIII BL guns in twin turrets 4 x 4in. Mk V QF guns in single mounts 2 x single 2-pdrs 6 x 21in. torpedoes in two triple mounts 2 x quad ½in. MGs
Wartime Modifications	
York	January 1940: 2 x single 20mm added.

HMS *LONDON* (1942) AND HMS *SUSSEX* (1943)

Before the war, HMS *London* (top) resembled all the other heavy cruisers of the County class. Then, during the extensive refit that lasted from March 1939 until February 1941, her two forward funnels were trunked together, she received a new bridge structure and hangar, a large fixed catapult, new twin 4-inch guns, multiple pom-poms, improved gunnery directors and a suite of radars. The reconstruction proved a disaster as all this added weight placed such a strain on her hull that she required two more lengthy refits before these problems were rectified. In this plate she is depicted as she appeared when she emerged from the first of these refits in January 1942. For most of that year she operated in support of the Arctic convoys.

HMS *Sussex* (bottom) was another London class heavy cruiser, but like her sisters *Devonshire* and *Shropshire* she was spared the extensive reconstruction afforded to *London*. However, in September 1940 she was hit by bombs and capsized in her dock during a German bombing raid on Glasgow's docks, and so she remained in Clydebank until her repairs were completed in July 1942. After a short 'working up' period in Scapa Flow and a spell with the Home Fleet she was sent to join the British forces gathering in the Indian Ocean. In this view *Sussex* is depicted as she appeared in August 1943, when she became the flagship of the Eastern Fleet.

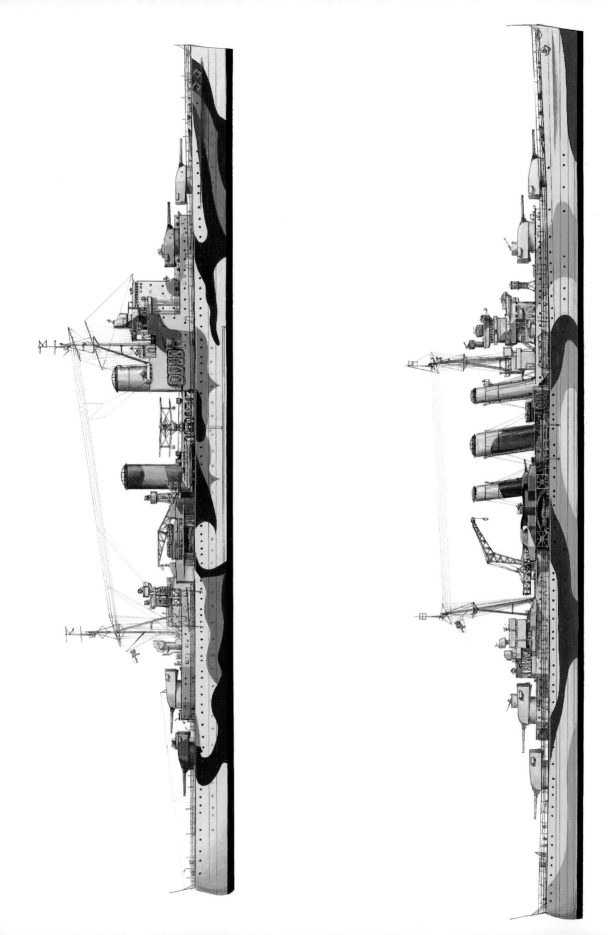

London Class

Displacement	9,850 tons (standard)
Dimensions Length Beam Draught	632ft 8in. overall 66ft 20ft 9in.
Propulsion	4 Parsons turbines, 8 Admiralty boilers, producing 80,000shp
Maximum speed	32kn
Fuel oil capacity	3,190 tons
Range	9,120 miles at 12kn
Aircraft	One (Walrus) – two occasionally carried
Armour Belt Decks Turrets	1in. 1–4½in. around magazines 1in.
Complement	784 officers and men
Armament	
Devonshire, *London,* *Shropshire, Sussex*	8 x 8in. Mk VIII BL guns in twin turrets 8 x 4in. Mk V QF guns in single mounts 2 x 8-barrelled 2-pdrs 8 x 21in. torpedoes in 2 quadruple mounts 2 x quad ½in. MGs
Wartime Modifications	
Devonshire	May 1941: 2 x 8-barrelled 2-pdr pom-pom and 2 x single 20mm added; Type 281 radar added. February 1942: 4 x single 20mm added; Type 273 radar added. December 1943: 2 x 8in. guns removed ('X' Turret); single 4in. replaced by twin 4in. mounts; 2 x single 20mm added. January 1944: quad MGs and 6 x single 20mm removed; 2 x quad 2-pdr pom-pom and 12 x twin 20mm added; aircraft and catapult removed, Type 282, 283, 285 radars added. October 1944: 8-barrelled pom-poms replaced by quad pom-poms; 5 x twin 20mm removed, 10 x single 20mm added.
London	January 1941: single 4in. guns replaced by 2 x 4in. guns in twin mounts; Type 279, 284 and 285 radars added. December 1941: quad MGs removed; 8 x single 20mm added; Type 273 and 282 radars added. April 1943: aircraft and catapult removed, 7 x single 20mm added. January 1944: 4 x twin and 1 x single 20mm added.
Shropshire	April 1941: 2 x 8-barrelled 2-pdr pom-poms added. December 1941: 8 x single 4in. guns replaced by 4 x twin 4in. guns; 7 x single 20mm added; Type 273, 281, 282 and 285 radars added. December 1942: 3 x single 20mm added.
As HMAS *Shropshire*	May 1943: 6 x single 20mm removed; 7 x twin 20mm added; aircraft, catapult and quad MGs removed. June 1944: 4 x single 20mm added. May 1945: 13 x single 40mm Bofors added; 2 x single 20mm and 5 x twin 20mm removed; Type 273 radar removed; Type 277 and 293 radars added; torpedo tubes removed.
Sussex	April 1940: UP Projectors fitted. July 1942: UP Projectors and quad MGs removed; 8 x single 4in. guns replaced by 4 x twin 4in. guns; 2 x 8-barrelled 2-pdr pom-poms and 10 x single 20mm added; Type 273, 281, 282 and 285 radars added. November 1943: 12 x single 20mm added; aircraft and catapult removed. December 1944: 2 x 8in. guns ('X' turret) and torpedo tubes removed; 15 x single 20mm removed; 4 x twin 20mm and 2 x quad 2-pdr pom-poms added.

Norfolk Class

Displacement	9,975 tons (standard)
Dimensions Length Beam Draught	 632ft 8in. overall 66ft 20ft 11in.
Propulsion	4 Parsons turbines, 8 Admiralty boilers, producing 80,000shp
Maximum speed	32kn
Fuel oil capacity	3,190 tons
Range	12,500 miles at 12kn
Aircraft	One (Walrus)
Armour Belt Decks Turrets	 1in. 1–4½in. around magazines 1in.
Complement	784 officers and men

Armament

Dorsetshire, Norfolk	8 x 8in. Mk VIII BL guns in twin turrets 8 x 4in. Mk V QF guns in 4 x twin mounts 2 x 8-barrelled 2-pdrs 8 x 21in. torpedoes in 2 quadruple mounts 2 x quad ½in. MGs

Wartime Modifications

Dorsetshire	July 1941: 9 x single 20mm added.
Norfolk	May 1940: 2 UP projectors added. October 1940: Type 286M radar fitted. August 1941: UP projectors and quad MGs removed; 6 x single 20mm added, type 273, 281, 284 and 285 radars added. October 1942: 3 x single 20mm added; Type 273 radar added; aircraft and catapult removed. May 1943: 9 x single 20mm added. November 1944: 2 x 8in. guns ('X' turret) removed; 2 x 8-barrelled pom-poms replaced by 6 x quad 2-pdr pom-poms; 2 x single 20mm removed; 11 x twin 20mm added; all but Type 285 radar removed; Type 274, 277, 282, 283 and 293 radars added. September 1945: 10 x single 20mm replaced by 10 x single 40mm Bofors.

HMS *Cumberland* as she appeared in late February 1942, while serving with the Home Fleet. The dark-grey hull and light-grey upperworks scheme shown in Plate A was replaced by a more complex disruptive pattern before this three-tone grey scheme was adopted in October 1941.

HMS *London* pictured in May 1943, after emerging from a second major refit in Tyneside, which rectified most of the structural problems caused by her rebuilding in 1939–41. Her appearance was unique among the heavy cruisers of the County class.

Exeter Class

Displacement	8,390 tons (standard)
Dimensions Length Beam Draught	575ft overall 58ft 20ft 3in.
Propulsion	4 Parsons turbines, 8 Admiralty boilers, producing 80,000shp
Maximum speed	32kn
Fuel oil capacity	1,900 tons
Range	10,000 miles at 14kn
Aircraft	Two (Walrus)
Armour Belt Deck Turrets	1in. 1–5in. around magazines 1in.
Complement	628 officers and men
Armament	
Exeter	6 x 8in. Mk VIII BL guns in twin turrets 4 x 4in. Mk V QF guns in single mounts 2 x single 2-pdrs 6 x 21in. torpedoes in two triple mounts 2 x quad ½in. MGs
Wartime Modifications	
Exeter	March 1940: 4 x single 4in. guns replaced by 4 x twin 4in. guns; 2 x single 2-pdrs replaced by 2 x 8-barrelled 2-pdr pom-poms; Type 279 radar added; 2 x single 20mm added.

 HMS *BERWICK* AT THE BATTLE OF CAPE SPARTIVENTO, 1940

HMS *Berwick* was a Kent class heavy cruiser that saw service in the Atlantic and the Norwegian Sea before being sent to Gibraltar to join Force H in late 1940. On 27 November she took part in a surface action against the Italian Fleet, operating as part of the 18th Cruiser Squadron, under the command of Vice-Admiral Holland, who flew his flag in HMS *Manchester*. The other four cruisers of this force carried 6-inch guns, so when the enemy was sighted Holland ordered them to close the distance to bring their guns within range. They advanced in line abreast, with *Berwick* formed up on the starboard side of the formation. Their opponents were Italian heavy cruisers and initially only *Berwick's* 8-inch guns could match their range, although the light cruisers fired their guns to unnerve the enemy. The accuracy of the Italian gunnery was surprisingly good; *Berwick* was straddled and then hit, as an 8-inch shell knocked out 'Y' turret.

The plate shows *Berwick* at the start of the action. The flagship *Manchester* was sailing abreast of her, and with (in order) *Newcastle*, *Southampton* and *Sheffield* deployed on the flagship's port beam. The Italian cruisers have found her range, but *Berwick* is returning their fire.

The London class heavy cruiser HMS *Devonshire*, as she appeared in 1942, while operating in the Indian Ocean. The unofficial two-colour disruptive scheme she had carried since early 1940 had faded to produce this shabby appearance, which she retained until May 1943.

SERVICE HISTORY, 1939–45

Hawkins Class

HMS *Effingham*

Effingham was part of the 12th Cruiser Squadron when the war broke out and she served in the Northern Patrol before being detached in November to transport gold to Canada, to pay for American war materials. She spent the opening months of 1940 hunting German raiders in the North Atlantic, but following the German invasion of Norway she was ordered to join Allied naval forces off Narvik. She fired in support of Allied troops there and was transporting reinforcements from Harstad to Bodo when on 18 April she struck a submerged rock. Damaged beyond repair, *Effingham* was sunk by gunfire three days later.

HMS *Frobisher*

Frobisher spent the early years of the war in refit in Portsmouth, but in January 1942 she was recommissioned and after a brief secondment with the Home Fleet was ordered to escort a convoy bound for South Africa. Reaching Durban in June, she performed escort duties in the Indian Ocean before joining the Eastern Fleet in Colombo (in Ceylon, now Sri Lanka). She remained in Far Eastern waters until March 1944, when she returned to Britain. After undergoing repairs in Greenock *Frobisher* sailed south to take part in the Normandy landings, providing gunfire support off Sword Beach. After suffering minor damage from bombs and torpedoes she was repaired in Rosyth, where she remained until the end of the war.

HMS *Exeter*, as she appeared before the outbreak of World War II. During the battle of the River Plate in December 1939 all three of her 8-inch gun turrets were put out of action, while her open bridge and director control tower were also hit.

HMS *Hawkins*

Hawkins spent the first months of the war undergoing a refit in Portsmouth, but in January 1940 she was dispatched to the South Atlantic to hunt for German raiders. She remained there until September, when she put in to Durban for a refit. In February she operated off Italian Somaliland, intercepting enemy transports and bombarding shore positions. She remained in the Indian Ocean until November 1942, hunting for enemy raiders and escorting convoys. December saw her returned to Portsmouth and after a six-month refit *Hawkins* joined the Home Fleet for two months of trials, then headed back to the Indian Ocean. She remained in the region until March 1944, when she was recalled to Britain. After undergoing repairs on the Clyde she took part in the Normandy landings, providing support for American troops off Utah Beach. By the end of June she returned to the Clyde for a refit and she was still there when hostilities ended.

Kent Class
HMS *Berwick*

Berwick was in the Caribbean when war was declared and she spent the first six months of the conflict escorting convoys or hunting German raiders in the Atlantic. In April 1940 she participated in the Norwegian campaign and remained with the Home Fleet until November, when she joined Force H based in Gibraltar. She was slightly damaged at the battle of Cape Spartivento (27 November 1940), . She was damaged again on Christmas Day, when she encountered the German heavy cruiser *Admiral Hipper* off the Azores. After repairs in Britain were completed in June 1941 she joined the Home Fleet and spent the rest of the war escorting Arctic convoys.

HMS *Cumberland* pictured during a visit to Malta in late 1945, while returning home after her service with the Eastern Fleet. During the last year of the war she operated in the Indian Ocean and the East Indies.

HMS *Dorsetshire* at anchor in Scapa Flow in August 1941. *Berwick* is anchored off her port beam, while *Furious* can be seen ahead of her. During 1941–42 she was painted in this simple two-colour mid- and light-grey disruptive camouflage scheme.

The Type B heavy cruiser HMS *York*, photographed in 1933, while she was serving on the America and West Indies station. She can readily be distinguished from *Exeter* by her older-style tiered bridge structure. She retained her pre-war paint scheme until 1940.

HMS *Cornwall*

Cornwall formed part of the 5th Cruiser Squadron based on the China station, and when hostilities began she remained in Eastern waters as part of Force I based in Ceylon. She took part in the hunt for the *Graf Spee*, then joined the South Atlantic command. After participating in operations against the Vichy French at Dakar in West Africa (August 1940), she then remained off the African coast, hunting down Vichy French stragglers. In early 1941 she returned to the Indian Ocean, where she destroyed the German raider *Pinguin* (May 1941). After Japan's entry into the war she served with the Eastern Fleet based in Ceylon, until 5 April 1942, when she was attacked and sunk by Japanese aircraft off the Maldive Islands. A total of 191 of her crew were lost when she sank.

HMS *Cumberland*

When the war began, *Cumberland* was operating off South America and participated in operations against the *Graf Spee*. She narrowly missed participating in the battle of the River Plate, but remained in the Atlantic throughout 1940, hunting raiders, escorting convoys and enforcing blockades of neutral ports. She also took part in the action off Dakar, when she was slightly damaged. Joining the Home Fleet in early 1941, she spent the next three years escorting Arctic convoys. March 1944 saw her join the Eastern Fleet and she remained in Far Eastern waters until the end of the war, serving as an escort for the British carrier force.

HMS *Kent*

Kent was in the Far East when war was declared and she remained there until January 1940, hunting German raiders. She then acted as a convoy escort in the Indian Ocean before joining the Mediterranean Fleet in June 1940. Participating in the bombardment of Bardia (August 1940), she was damaged the following month by an Italian aerial torpedo and sent home for repairs. She was recommissioned in September 1941, and after trials joined the Home Fleet. She escorted Arctic convoys until January 1945, when she was placed in reserve.

HMS *Suffolk*

Suffolk returned home from the Far East when the war began, to serve with the Home Fleet. By October she was on patrol in the Denmark Straits between Iceland and Greenland, where she remained until April 1940, when she participated in the Norway campaign. On 17 April she was badly damaged by German aircraft while operating off Stavanger and limped home to be repaired. By February 1941 she was back in service and resumed her place in the Denmark Straits in time to shadow the *Bismarck* during her infamous sortie in May. She remained with the Home Fleet until December 1942, when she underwent a refit. In April 1943 she was dispatched to join the Eastern Fleet and she served in the Indian Ocean until the end of the war.

HMS *Frobisher* was placed in reserve and served as a training ship between the wars, but she was re-armed and sent to the Far East. She returned home in time to fire her guns in support of the Normandy landings.

London Class

HMS *Devonshire*

Devonshire began the war in the Mediterranean and was immediately transferred to the Home Fleet. She participated in the Norwegian campaign in April 1940 and by August she was off Dakar in West Africa, taking part in operations against the Vichy French. She remained in the South Atlantic until she returned home for a refit in February 1941. *Devonshire* rejoined the Home Fleet in May and was on hand to join the hunt for the *Bismarck*. Remaining with the Home Fleet until September, she was subsequently ordered to African waters. She performed well, capturing a Vichy French convoy and the German raider *Atlantis*. After a three-month refit in Norfolk, Virginia (January to March 1942) she returned to the Indian Ocean and served with the Eastern Fleet until April 1943. From May 1943 until March 1944 she underwent a refit in Britain, then spent the last year of the war with the Home Fleet.

HMS *London*

London was undergoing a major reconstruction in Chatham, Kent when the war began, and entered service again only in February 1941. She operated in the Atlantic, participating in the search for the *Bismarck* in April and then in the subsequent hunt for her supply ships. By that time problems caused by her reconstruction had become apparent and she returned to Britain for another major refit in October 1941. She re-emerged the following January, when she joined the Home Fleet, escorting Arctic convoys until December 1942 when she returned home for yet another refit. In May 1943 she was recommissioned and sent to join the Eastern Fleet. She remained in the Far East until the end of the war.

HMS *Shropshire*

Shropshire was in the Mediterranean Fleet when the war began but was soon ordered into the Atlantic and the Indian Ocean to join the hunt for German raiders, including the *Graf Spee*. After a brief refit in Simonstown in South Africa she was used as a convoy escort in the Atlantic, before returning to Clydeside for a full refit in June 1940. In August she returned to Simonstown and spent the next year in the Indian Ocean, escorting convoys and supporting land operations in Somaliland. After another refit in Simonstown (March to June 1941) she returned home for a major refurbishment, before being transferred to the Royal Australian Navy in April 1943 as HMAS *Shropshire*. She spent the remainder of the war in Far Eastern waters, under the Australian flag.

HMS *Sussex*

Sussex was detached from the Mediterranean Fleet shortly after the outbreak of war and sent into the South Atlantic and Indian Ocean to join the hunt for the *Graf Spee* and other German raiders. She returned to Britain in March 1940 and took part in the Norwegian campaign in April. After an engineering defect was noticed in August she was sent to Clydebank for repairs but on 17 September she was struck by a bomb during a German air raid and capsized in her flooded dry dock. Repairs lasted until July 1942, when she rejoined the Home Fleet. In November she underwent a minor refit before sailing to the Far East in February 1943; on her passage out she intercepted a German tanker in the Atlantic. From March until October she served as a convoy

A spirited Italian propaganda poster, showing the successful attack on HMS *York* in Crete's Suda Bay on 26 March 1941 by a one-man Italian MTM explosive motor boat. The courageous pilot abandoned his craft seconds before it struck the cruiser.

escort in the Indian Ocean, and in March 1944, after another refit in Simonstown, she joined the main Eastern Fleet in Ceylon. She remained in the Far East until the end of the war, spending much of her time supporting Allied operations in the Dutch East Indies.

HMS Kent pictured in Plymouth Sound in September 1941, after emerging from a refit. She is painted in a four-colour camouflage scheme of mid-grey, light grey, dark grey and grey-blue, a scheme she retained with minor variants until 1944.

Norfolk Class
HMS Norfolk

Norfolk was in refit when the war began but she hurriedly joined the Home Fleet and helped blockade the Denmark Straits. On 15 March 1940 she was damaged during a German bombing raid on Scapa Flow and sent south to Clydeside for repairs. She rejoined the fleet in June, when she resumed operations with the Northern Patrol. In December she was sent into the South Atlantic to hunt for German raiders, including the *Admiral Scheer* and the *Kormoran*. By February 1941 she was being used as a convoy escort, but she rejoined the Home Fleet in May and was in the Denmark Straits when the *Bismarck* made her sortie later that month. After the battle of the Denmark Straits she shadowed the German battleship and was present when the *Bismarck* was finally sunk on 27 May. From July to September 1941 she underwent a refit in Tyneside and then rejoined the Home Fleet, when she was deployed as an escort for the Arctic convoys. She took part in the disastrous PQ17 convoy operation and remained in Arctic waters throughout 1942–43, apart from a brief foray to escort American troop convoys to North Africa in October 1942. In December 1943 she saw action against the *Scharnhorst* in the battle of North Cape, when she was hit twice. After repairs in Tyneside (when 'X' turret was removed) she remained with the Home Fleet until the end of the war.

HMS *Dorsetshire*

Dorsetshire was on the China station when the war began, but she was ordered west into the Indian Ocean to hunt for German raiders, including the *Graf Spee*. In January 1940 she escorted the damaged cruiser *Exeter* home from the Falklands, but returned to South American waters to resume the hunt for German supply ships. After a brief refit in Simonstown (May) she returned to Britain for another refit before joining British forces off Dakar in West Africa. After a brief sojourn in the Indian Ocean to support Allied troops in Somaliland she resumed patrolling in the South Atlantic, operating from South African ports. From December 1940 until April 1941 she was occupied escorting convoys off the Atlantic coast of Africa, but in May was diverted northwards to participate in the hunt for the *Bismarck*. On 27 May she finished the stricken German battleship off with her torpedoes, although by then the *Bismarck's* crew may already have detonated scuttling charges, and *Dorsetshire* merely helped her on her way. Afterwards she returned to trade protection off Africa and escorted convoys across the Indian Ocean. In February 1942 she arrived in Ceylon to join the Eastern Fleet, after undergoing a brief refit in Colombo. On 5 April 1942 she was in company with HMS *Cornwall* off the Maldives when she was attacked and sunk by Japanese carrier-borne aircraft. A total of 234 of her crew lost their lives in the attack.

York Class
HMS *York*

York was on her way to Halifax, Nova Scotia when the war began, and after providing an escort for an Atlantic convoy she was used to hunt for German raiders in the Caribbean and Western Atlantic. She escorted another convoy home to Britain in December, then underwent a refit in Liverpool until January. She joined the Home Fleet and in April 1940 participated in the Norwegian campaign. She remained in northern waters until August, when she was transferred to the Mediterranean Fleet. She saw action off Greece on 13 October, when she sank an Italian destroyer, and in November she provided cover for the Fleet Air Arm attack on Taranto. She remained in the Eastern Mediterranean for several months, escorting convoys from Alexandria to Malta and Greece. In early March 1941 she was sent to Suda Bay in Crete, and it was there on 26 March she was badly damaged in an attack by Italian explosive motor boats. She had to be beached in shallow water and was still there on 18 May when she was crippled by bombs during an air attack. *York* was finally scuttled using explosives on 22 May when the British were forced to evacuate Crete.

 HMS *EXETER* AT THE BATTLE OF THE RIVER PLATE, 1939

Shortly after dawn on 13 December 1939, lookouts on board HMS *Exeter* sighted the German pocket battleship *Graf Spee* to the north-west. Captain Bell steered towards the enemy, hoping to close the range as quickly as possible, so his guns might have a chance of penetrating its armour. Bell's superior, Admiral Harwood in HMS *Ajax*, accompanied by HMS *Achilles*, steamed to the north in order to split the German fire. *Graf Spee* opened fire at 6.18am, followed two minutes later by *Exeter*, firing at a range of 19,400 yards (just under 10 nautical miles). The two British light cruisers joined in minutes later. German gunnery proved highly accurate and *Exeter* was straddled by the *Graf Spee's* third salvo. Splinters from German fire destroyed *Exeter's* aircraft and killed the crew of one of her torpedo mounts. For her part *Exeter* was firing quickly and also straddled the enemy with her third salvo.

Then at around 6.25am an 11-inch shell from the *Graf Spee* struck *Exeter's* 'B' turret, putting it out of action. Shell splinters also riddled her director control tower, her bridge and her conning position. A wounded Captain Bell worked his way aft to fight his ship from the secondary conning position, but *Exeter* was hit twice more in as many minutes and was badly damaged. 'A' turret was now put out of action, and flooding would soon force 'Y' turret to cease fire. Fortunately for Bell and his crew, the Germans then switched their fire to the light cruisers, and *Exeter* was able to disengage from the fight.

The plate shows *Exeter* around 6.23am, when she was straddled by German fire. Her own guns are firing at a high elevation, trained over the starboard bow. She is flying several battle ensigns, which she continued to display throughout the brief action. *Ajax* and *Achilles* can be seen in the background, set against the rising sun.

Exeter Class

HMS *Exeter*

Exeter was patrolling off the Atlantic coast of South America when hostilities began, and she was ordered to form part of Force G, hunting for German raiders in South American waters. On 13 August she played a leading role in the battle of the River Plate, when she and her consorts *Ajax* and *Achilles* drove the German pocket battleship *Graf Spee* into the neutral port of Montevideo. She was badly damaged during the action and suffered significant casualties – 63 dead and 23 wounded. After temporary repairs in the Falklands she returned to Gosport, where she underwent a major refit (March 1940 to March 1941). In May she was deployed as a convoy escort in the Atlantic and the Indian Ocean, but following Japan's entry into the war she was sent to Singapore. January 1942 saw her transfer to the joint Allied task force known as American-British-Dutch-Australian Command (ABDA), and was sent to defend the Dutch East Indies from Japanese invasion. Instead on 27 February ABDA was engaged and defeated by a Japanese cruiser force in the battle of the Java Sea. *Exeter* was badly damaged in the battle and was sent to Colombo for repairs. On 1 March she was intercepted by a Japanese task force and sunk by gunfire and torpedoes. Of her crew, 54 were killed in the action and 651 were taken prisoner.

ARMAMENT AND OPERATION

Britain's wartime heavy cruisers were a product of their time. Built during the 1920s, they were designed to fight the previous war, and to guard the sea lanes that bound the Empire together. Thanks to the limitations of the Washington Navy Treaty they lacked protection and carried fewer heavy guns than some of their naval rivals. For instance, the US Northampton class laid down in the late 1920s carried nine 8-inch guns each, mounted in three triple turrets. While Japanese heavy cruisers of the early 1920s carried just six 8-inch guns, which made them comparable to *Exeter* and *York*, the Nachi and Takao classes built during the later 1920s all carried ten 8-inch guns, in twin turrets. While French and Italian cruisers of the same period carried a similar armament to the County class cruisers, their ships tended to be sleeker and faster than their British counterparts.

Still, these were all vessels that were built within the restrictions of the treaty and for the most part they sacrificed armour to achieve what their designers and naval chiefs wanted. In Britain's case the County class was primarily a vessel designed to hunt down enemy raiders, and so the DNCs emphasized range and reliability over almost all other considerations. Given this requirement, these British heavy cruisers did everything that was asked of them. During World War II they spent much of their time searching for enemy raiders, protecting convoys from attacks by enemy surface warships and generally fulfilling the expectations of their designers. What changed, of course, was that these warships had to operate in a naval environment that was very different from the one that had existed when they were first planned. The threat posed by enemy aircraft had increased dramatically during the late 1930s and so these warships were modified accordingly. Those that survived the war – and most of them did – bristled with small-calibre anti-aircraft weapons and enjoyed the advantages offered by fire control and search radars. While not initially designed to fight a modern conflict, they soon became efficient and effective fighting ships, worthy of their place in the wartime fleet.

Main Armament

With the exception of the Hawkins class, all British heavy cruisers carried the same main armament of 8-inch Mark VIII breech-loading (BL) guns. The only difference between them was in the mountings, as Kent class and London class vessels had Mark I mountings, while the Norfolk class plus *York* and *Exeter* had Mark II versions.

While the gun itself was both reliable and accurate, its method of mounting was overly ambitious. In the Mark I mount the gun was capable of being elevated to 70°, when a 42° elevation was all that was needed to fire a shell out to the guns' maximum range of 29,000 yards (just short of 15 nautical miles). There were also problems with the hydraulics, which could train the gun at a speed of 8° a second, and elevate it even faster, but which made it difficult to position the barrel accurately. It was well into the 1930s before a more accurate hydraulic system was used, which immediately improved both accuracy and speed of operation.

In all British heavy cruisers the magazines and shell rooms were on the same deck. Charges were passed from the magazine to the handling room

The high freeboard of the County class cruiser is clearly shown in this view of HMS *Suffolk*, riding high in the water due to her near-empty fuel oil tanks. She is sporting the three-tone Admiralty-pattern camouflage scheme she wore during her deployment with the Eastern Fleet in 1944.

F HMS *CORNWALL* (1942)

The Kent class heavy cruiser HMS *Cornwall* was in the Far East when war broke out and so it was not until July 1940 that she returned to Britain for repairs and a refit. However, few modifications were made and essentially she remained unaltered since her last pre-war refit in 1936–37. She then spent the remainder of the war in the Indian Ocean, or operating off the African coast. Then, on 5 April 1942 she and her consort *Dorsetshire* were attacked to the east of Ceylon by 50 Japanese aircraft launched from three Japanese aircraft carriers. *Cornwall* was struck repeatedly and sank within minutes.

HMS *Cornwall*

Kent class heavy cruiser

Displacement: 10,900 tons (standard)

Dimensions: Length: 630ft overall Beam: 68ft 5in. Draught: 20ft 6in.

Propulsion: 4 Parsons turbines, 8 Admiralty boilers, producing 80,000shp
(Note: *Berwick* fitted with Brown-Curtis turbines)

Maximum speed: 31½kn

Fuel oil capacity: 3,424 tons

Range: 9,350 miles at 12kn

Armament:

  8 x 8in. Mk VIII BL guns in twin turrets;
  8 x 4in. Mk V QF guns in twin mounts;
  6 x 4in. in 2 single and 2 twin mounts;
  2 x quad 2-pdr pom-poms
  8 x 21in. torpedoes in two quadruple mounts (not *Cumberland*)
  2 x quad ½in. MGs

Aircraft: Two (Walrus)

Armour: Belt: 1in. Decks: 1–4½in. around magazines Turrets: 1in.

Complement: 784 officers and men

Key

1. 'A' turret (2 x 8In. guns)
2. 'B' turret
3. Upper bridge (open)
4. Gunnery control tower
5. Foremast
6. Twin 4in. gun (1 of 4)
7. Quad 2-pdr pom-pom (1 of 2)
8. Cranes (port and starboard)
9. Whaler
10. Ship's motor boats
11. Wireless aerials
12. 36in. searchlights
13. Secondary gun director
14. Quad-mounted machine guns
15. Mainmast
16. Catapult
17. Hangar for Walrus floatplane
18. 'X' turret
19. 'Y' turret
20. Quarterdeck
21. Turbine room
22. Boiler room
23. Ventilators
24. Traversing ring
25. Magazine
26. Shell room
27. Handling room
28. Barbette
29. Working chamber
30. Gun house

HMS *Berwick* in Scapa Flow, adding her weight to the flak barrage during an air defence exercise at the fleet anchorage in early 1942. The previous year she had been painted in a 'Mountbatten Pink' camouflage scheme.

through revolving scuttles, and placed on trays fitted to the shell hoist. Each gun had its own hoist, and each hoist had two cages, which allowed one to be loading in the handling room while the other was being used in the turret to load the guns. Shells were moved using overhead gantries, both in the shell room and in the turret. In the shell room a hydraulic ring held 30 upright shells, ready to be hoisted up to the turret when required. Once there, the shells were deposited on to shell tilting trays, and a hydraulic rammer would then insert both the shell and the propellant charge into the breech. The whole loading and firing operation could be carried out in 11 seconds.

The Mark II mountings used in Norfolk class and Class B cruisers had their maximum elevation reduced to 50°, as the overambitious anti-aircraft

8in. Breech Loader, Mk VIII

Calibre	8in.	Rate of fire	Five rounds per minute
Date of design	1921	Weight of shell	256lb
Date first in service	1927	Shell types	High explosive; armour piercing
Length of bore	50 calibres (400in.)	Weight of propellant charge	66lb ('supercharge')
Length of barrel	413in.	Muzzle velocity	2,805fps
Weight of gun	17.2 tons	Maximum range	30,650 yards
Mounting	Twin Mk I or Mk II	Ammunition storage per gun	150 rounds
Maximum elevation	70° (50° in Mk II mounts)	Estimated barrel life before replacement	550 rounds

Range and velocity (given for armour-piercing shells)

Gun elevation	Range	Strike velocity (feet per second)	Angle of descent	Flight time
3°	5,000 yards	2,154fps	2.5°	6 seconds
5°	10,000 yards	1,683fps	7°	14 seconds
10°	15,000 yards	1,322fps	15.75°	25 seconds
16.5°	20,000 yards	1,169fps	28.5°	39 seconds
26.75°	25,000 yards	1,164fps	56°	56 seconds
41.5°	29,000 yards	1,240fps	79°	79 seconds

capability of the Mark I mounts was abandoned. While the shell room capacity was less than in the earlier turrets, the guns were served by a more efficient system based around an endless-band conveyor, and it made better use of the space available within the shell room and turret (or 'gunhouse'). In operational terms there was no notable difference between the two types of mountings and both performed well in action. The greatest liability of the whole design was the thin 1-inch thick armour of the turret itself, and of the director control tower. With such poor protection, the guns were vulnerable to damage from enemy fire, and on several occasions 8-inch turrets were knocked out by enemy hits that might have been deflected if the turrets had been adequately protected.

The 7½-inch guns used in Hawkins class cruisers were operated in a similar manner, but the guns themselves only had a maximum range of 21,110 yards, and a striking velocity of 1,078fps, fired at the maximum elevation of a single Mark V mounting of 30°. At that range the angle of descent was just over 46°, making it less effective than the plunging fire of the 8-inch gun, which dropped almost vertically at maximum range. Their rate of fire was also considerably slower, at around three rounds per minute. By 1939, only *Frobisher* and *Hawkins* still carried their main 7½-inch guns, still mounted in their original open-backed turrets.

Anti-Aircraft Armament

The singly mounted 4-inch quick-firing (QF) guns initially carried on these cruisers were designed primarily as anti-aircraft (AA) weapons. These were 'High Angle' (HA) guns, with a maximum elevation of 80°. That allowed them to engage aircraft flying at 31,000 feet, and gave them a maximum surface range of 16,430 yards (just over 8 nautical miles). These weapons were first introduced in 1914 and, while still used in heavy AA batteries sited around London, they were considered obsolete by 1939.

They were gradually replaced by the 4-inch QF Mark XVI, mounted in

The crew of a quadruple 2-pdr pom-pom QF Mark VII at the alert on board a British heavy cruiser operating in home waters during 1940. These multi-barrelled weapons threw up a curtain of fire to deter low-flying attacking aircraft.

twin Mark XIX mounts. These guns had a better performance than their predecessors and could hit aircraft at 39,000 feet, or surface targets out to 19,850 yards. However, their real advantages lay in their improved accuracy, velocity and rate of fire. The introduction of radar-guided fire control systems also made these weapons even more effective. As anti-aircraft guns these large-calibre weapons had their limitations, but their real value lay in putting up a wall of flak, designed to protect a task force. These guns proved their worth as barrage weapons throughout the war.

All the heavy cruisers that survived long enough were given increasing numbers of small-calibre anti-aircraft weapons as the war wore on. Initially, AA protection was afforded by Vickers 2-pdr QF pom-poms on single mounts, or by Vickers ½-inch machine guns on quadruple mountings. Both weapons were designed before World War I, when aircraft were not considered a practical threat to large warships. By 1939 they were both outdated, as they lacked the stopping power or longevity of firepower needed to deter attacks by modern bombers. They were eventually replaced by either multiple pom-poms or 20mm Oerlikons. Four-barrelled or eight-barrelled pom-poms threw up an impressive volume of fire and proved useful against both dive-bombers and torpedo-bombers. The eight-barrelled versions were first developed in the early 1920s, while the lighter and more flexible quad versions appeared during the mid-1930s.

The 20mm Oerlikon was a great improvement on the earlier ½-inch machine gun and it proved highly effective. It became even more useful later in the war, when twin mounted versions were introduced, in powered mountings. These allowed the gunner to track aircraft, and with a ceiling of 10,000 feet they were ideally suited to counter Stukas – the greatest aerial threat the Royal Navy faced during the war. Later in the war many of these 20mm mounts were replaced by 40mm Bofors QF guns – probably the most effective British AA gun of the war. They proved their worth against the Japanese, as they were powerful enough to destroy an oncoming kamikaze plane before it reached the target ship.

Other Weaponry

The best British torpedo of World War I was the 21-inch Mark V, which had a range of 13,500 yards at 25 knots. These were the torpedoes that were used

 HMS *EXETER* (1942) AND HMS *FROBISHER* (1942)

In the eight years between entering service and the battle of the River Plate in 1939, HMS *Exeter* (top) received only minor improvements – the addition of a pair of quad machine-gun mounts and small modifications to her engines. However, after the battle she received new twin 4-inch gun mounts, eight-barrelled pom-poms replaced her machine guns, and her two small fixed catapults were replaced by a single large turntable version. Just as importantly, she was fitted with a Type 279 air warning radar. Unusually, she was never repainted in Admiralty disruptive scheme camouflage, but retained her pre-war coat of mid-grey until she was sunk in action on 1 May 1942. Her wooden decks also remained unpainted. This view shows her as she looked during the battle of the Java Sea in February 1942.

By contrast HMS *Frobisher* (bottom) began the war as a partly disarmed training ship but after a much-delayed refit she was re-armed, and re-commissioned in March 1942. In her resurrected condition she carried five of her original 7½-inch guns and was given an adequate anti-aircraft capability in the form of single 4-inch guns, multiple pom-poms and 20mm Oerlikons. She was also fitted with a full suite of air warning, surface search and fire control radars. This view of *Frobisher* shows her as she appeared in the summer of 1942, when she began two years of service with the Eastern Fleet, operating in the Indian Ocean.

Before her refit in 1940, HMS *Exeter* was unusually fitted with two fixed catapults, fitted at an angle of 35° to the hull. These took up less space than the larger centreline rotating catapult she was fitted with in 1941–42.

in the Kent class, but the long drop from the upper deck led to them breaking up on impact with the water. A new version was produced with a strengthened tail and the problem went away. The 21-inch Mark VIII torpedo replaced this earlier model on some London and Norfolk class cruisers during the war, which lacked the long range of its predecessor (its maximum range was 7,000 yards), but it had a speed of up to 45 knots and was significantly more reliable. Torpedoes were carried in quadruple mounts in County class vessels, and triple mounts in Type B cruisers. In the Hawkins class torpedoes were carried in fixed above-water and submerged tubes, but these proved so ineffective that they were rarely operational. During the war the torpedoes and their mounts were eventually removed from almost all British heavy cruisers, as it was felt that the risk they presented to their own ships if the mount was hit far outweighed any benefits they might have as offensive weapons. This said, the *Dorsetshire* famously used her torpedoes to finish off the stricken German battleship *Bismarck*, although it has also been claimed that the battleship was sinking anyway by the time the cruiser launched her salvo.

A final weapon of sorts were the aircraft that were carried on all British heavy cruisers during the early years of the war. These were used to search for the enemy and to direct fall of shot. The first catapult on board a British warship was installed in 1923, and in 1926 it was decided to install these contraptions to some Hawkins class cruisers and all new 8-inch cruisers. At first distinctions were made between spotter-reconnaissance aircraft and smaller fighter-reconnaissance ones, but by the 1930s the Hawker Osprey, the Fairey IIIF and the Fairey Seal all proved equally effective – or ineffective. These frail machines lacked the range and robust design the Admiralty demanded, so they cast around for better aircraft. During the late 1930s, these cruisers were equipped with the Fairey Seafox and the larger Supermarine Seagull V ('Walrus') seaplanes, which proved far more suitable for naval operations.

Some vessels also experimented with the Fairey Swordfish, which combined its spotter-reconnaissance role with the ability to carry torpedoes. In the end it was the Walrus that proved the most effective type of aircraft for use on board these cruisers, despite the centreline space taken up by the large

A quadruple launcher for the 21-inch torpedo, of the kind fitted to all County class heavy cruisers during the early years of the war. By 1942–43 it was felt that these weapons were surplus to requirements and most mounts were removed.

rotating catapult it needed to launch. Some space was saved by designing these with retractable extensions, while on the *Exeter* two smaller fixed catapults proved just as effective. Wartime experience led to the realization that – like torpedo mountings – aircraft installations were dangerous. It was common to launch the aircraft before a cruiser engaged in battle, partly to help spot fall of shot, but also to reduce the risk of fire if the hangar was hit. Eventually, it was decided to do away with the aircraft installations altogether, although in most cases the hangar was retained. After all, radar could now do the same job and they didn't require highly flammable aviation fuel to function.

Radar

The first operational radar set – a Type 79Y air warning set – was first fitted on board a British cruiser in 1938. This led to the Type 279, followed by a better set, the Type 281 air warning radar, which entered service in 1940. This broad-beam air warning radar allowed British warships to detect aircraft at a range of 90–120 nautical miles, depending on altitude and atmospheric conditions. Its replacement, the Type 291 set, proved even more accurate. For surface targets, target identification radars such as Type 286 and 290 provided accurate targeting information as far as the horizon – usually about 40,000 yards (20 nautical miles). The surface warning sets Types 271, 272 and 273 introduced the plan position indicator (PPI) we associate with modern radar displays.

The next step was to use radar as a means of augmenting gunnery direction and fire control. The Type 282, fire control radar for short-range AA guns such as pom-poms was introduced in 1940, and was soon followed by the Type 285, which coordinated the fire of cruiser 4-inch guns. Main armament was guided by the Type 284M, the set used by *Suffolk* when it shadowed the *Bismarck* after the battle of the Denmark Strait. By 1942 an improved version – dubbed Type 284Q – was so effective that it allowed warships to direct their guns 'blind', using radar alone. This proved useful

The development of radar gave British warships a distinct tactical edge over their opponents. These radar operators pictured on board a British cruiser are manning a Type 279 air warning radar, which was also linked to the AA gun directors.

during the battle of North Cape (December 1943), when *Norfolk* found herself in action against the battle cruiser *Scharnhorst*. Other later war sets included the Type 277 air warning radar, and its Type 294 and 295 replacements, the Type 283 for directing secondary armament AA barrages, and the Type 275, a highly effective replacement for the Type 274. This radar capability gave British warships a distinct edge over their Italian, German and Japanese opponents, who generally lacked the sophisticated electronic array used by the Royal Navy. Knowing where the enemy was, and having the ability to hit him regardless of visibility more than compensated for the lack of armoured protection or the ageing hulls of Britain's fleet of heavy cruisers.

Effectiveness

To judge just how good these warships were, we need to consider their *raison d'être* – to guard the sea lanes, and to hunt down and destroy any enemy who threatened to interdict them. This is what these heavy cruisers were designed for and it was the role assigned to them for much of World War II. One of the first opportunities to demonstrate their effectiveness came during the hunt for the German pocket battleship *Graf Spee*. Between September and December 1939 she sank eight British merchantmen in the South Atlantic and one in the Indian Ocean. Of the eight Allied hunting groups sent to find her, three were French and six were British. These six British hunting groups included no fewer than eight British heavy cruisers – *Berwick*, *Cornwall*, *Cumberland*, *Dorsetshire*, *Exeter*, *Shropshire*, *Sussex* and *York*. However, it was *Exeter* that finally caught up with her in the River Plate on 13 December, accompanied by the light cruisers *Ajax* and *Achilles*.

The *Exeter* and the two light cruisers separated, to split the enemy's fire, and Captain Bell of the *Exeter* steamed directly towards the enemy, to close the range as quickly as possible. She was hit repeatedly, the first shot destroying her aircraft and wiping out the crew of a torpedo mount. Another 11-inch HE shell scored a direct hit on *Exeter's* 'B' turret, with its token 1 inch of armour. Shell splinters scoured her open bridge and ripped open her forecastle. What saved *Exeter* was the German Captain Langsdorff's decision to switch targets to the light cruisers and his decision to put in to neutral Montevideo. By the end of the action *Exeter's* 'A' turret had also been knocked out and a major firing was raging amidships. *Exeter* survived the battle, only to be sunk by Japanese cruisers in March 1942.

This vulnerability to enemy shot was also demonstrated during the battle of Cape Spartivento (27 November 1940), when *Berwick* and four light cruisers engaged five Italian heavy cruisers. The British advanced in line abreast, hoping to close the range as quickly as possible. The Italians opened fire at 22,000 yards (11 nautical miles), assisted by aircraft to spot their fall of shot. *Berwick* was bracketed by a salvo, and then hit, with an 8-inch shell ripping 'Y' turret apart. Twelve minutes later she was hit again in the stern, before the Italians pulled out of range. After the battle, one of *Berwick's* crew wrote, 'They say war is glamorous, but I was there when they opened up "Y" turret, and I don't want to see the like again.' The casualties in both actions were heavy, but so too was the loss of firepower due to a lack of armoured protection.

During the battle of the Denmark Strait *Norfolk* and *Suffolk* wisely avoided a duel with *Bismarck* and the modern heavy cruiser *Prinz Eugen*, but their radar reports proved invaluable and allowed the British to close in on the enemy until the Germans managed to break contact. This effective use of radar demonstrates another vital development, one that augmented the wartime role Britain gave her heavy cruisers. During the battle of North Cape (26 December 1943) *Norfolk* used her radar again, this time to detect the battle cruiser *Scharnhorst* before she could intercept an Allied convoy. Vice-Admiral Burnett (flying his flag in *Belfast*) used fire control radar to take the enemy by surprise, and *Norfolk* scored two hits on *Scharnhorst*, knocking out her radar and destroying her fire control director. Although the battle cruiser broke off the action, this lack of radar proved crucial, and allowed the British to eventually overhaul and destroy the *Scharnhorst*. Once again, just as she had when the *Bismarck* was sunk, *Norfolk* played her part in the final battle.

Apart from lack of armour (a problem shared by other cruisers of the same vintage), the real weakness of Britain's heavy cruisers during the first years of the war was their vulnerability to air attack. In April 1942 *Cornwall* and *Dorsetshire* were overwhelmed by Japanese carrier-borne aircraft and were sunk within minutes of each other. Off Norway and in the Mediterranean, other heavy cruisers were damaged by enemy bombs, or

HMS *Exeter* was damaged during the battle of the Java Sea (February 1942) but managed to limp to safety, only to be overhauled by a squadron of Japanese heavy cruisers on 1 March and forced to scuttle after an uneven fight.

This dramatic wartime drawing purports to show HMS *Dorsetshire* firing the torpedo that finally sank the German battleship *Bismarck* on 27 May 1941. It has since been argued that the *Bismarck's* crew were already scuttling their ship, and *Dorsetshire* merely hastened her end.

exposed to torpedo attacks. It was only when adequate close-range AA weapons were provided, and radar air warning and fire control systems were deployed, that these cruisers developed an adequate means of protecting themselves and the warships or merchantmen they were charged to protect.

We have described Britain's wartime heavy cruisers as warships of their time – vessels designed to conform to the limits of inter-war disarmament treaties, which were then subjected to the rigours of six years of war. For all their faults, these large, stately warships proved well suited to the task for which they had been designed. As guardians of the sea lanes, and as long-range hunters, they proved to be some of the most useful vessels in the Allied naval arsenal.

FURTHER READING

All the titles mentioned here are still available, either in bookshops or in good libraries. Many explore aspects of our subject in far more detail than has been possible in this short book and are therefore recommended as a source for further study.

Archibald, E.H.H., *The Fighting Ship in the Royal Navy, 1887–1984*, Blandford Press, Poole (1984)

Bennet, G, *The Battle of the River Plate*, Ian Allen Ltd, Shepperton (1972)

Brown, D.K., *The Design and Construction of British Warships, 1939–45: Volume 1: Major Surface Warships*, Conway Maritime Press, London (1995)

Campbell, John, *Naval Weapons of World War Two*, Arms and Armour Press, London (1990)

Friedman, Norman, *British Cruisers: Two World Wars and After*, Seaforth Publishing, Barnsley (2010)

Gardiner, Robert (ed.), *Conway's All the World's Fighting Ships, 1922–1946*, Conway Maritime Press, London (1980)

Gardiner, Robert (ed.), *Conway's All the World's Fighting Ships, 1906–1921*, Conway Maritime Press, London (1985)

Gardiner, Robert (ed.), *The Warship: The Eclipse of the Big Gun*, Conway Maritime Press, London (1992)

Greene, Jack & Massignani, Alessandro, *The Naval War in the Mediterranean, 1940–43*, Chatham Publishing, London (1989)

Konstam, Angus, *The Battle of North Cape*, Pen and Sword, Barnsley (2009)

Lavery, Brian, *Churchill's Navy: The Ships, Men and Organisation, 1939–1945*, Conway Maritime Press, London (2006)

Padfield, Peter, *Guns at Sea*, Evelyn Publishing, London (1973)

Raven, Alan & Roberts, John, *British Cruisers of World War Two*, Arms and Armour Press, London (1980)

Roberts, John, *British Warships of the Second World War*, Chatham Publishing, London, (2000)

Stephen, Martin, *British Warship Designs since 1906*, Ian Allen Ltd, Shepperton (1984)

Stephen, Martin, *Sea Battles in Close-up: World War 2*, Ian Allen Ltd, Shepperton (1988)

Whitley, M.J., *Cruisers of World War Two: An International Encyclopaedia*, Arms and Armour Press, London (1995)

Williams, Davis, *Naval Camouflage, 1914–1945: A Complete Visual Reference*, Chatham Publishing, London (2001)

HMS *Sussex*, wearing her pre-war mid-grey paint scheme, which she retained until she was bombed in September 1940. When she rejoined the fleet in August 1942 she was painted in a complex three-colour camouflage pattern (see Plate G).

INDEX

Illustrations are referred to in **bold**. For plates, the page number is in **bold**, followed by the caption locator in brackets, eg. **41** (40)